CW00470572

Shades of White

Country Living

Shades of White

HOW TO USE THE CLASSIC COLOR IN YOUR HOME

Edited by Caroline McKenzie

HEARST BOOKS

HEARSTBOOKS

An Imprint of Sterling Publishing Co., Inc.
1166 Avenue of the Americas
New York, NY 10036

ISBN 978-1-61837-290-1

Distributed in Canada by Sterling Publishing
c/o Canadian Manda Group, 664 Annette Street
Toronto, Ontario M6S 2C8, Canada
Distributed in Australia by NewSouth Books
University of New South Wales, Sydney, NSW 2052, Australia

For information about custom editions, special sales, and premium and corporate purchases, please contact Sterling Special Sales at 800-805-5489 or specialsales@sterlingpublishing.com.

Manufactured in Singapore

2 4 6 8 10 9 7 5 3

sterlingpublishing.com
countryliving.com

Interior design by Shannon Nicole Plunkett
Cover design by Elizabeth Mihaltse Lindy
Photography credits on page 180

Contents

Foliage House Plants
Annuals
Rock and Water Gardens
Flowering Shrubs
Landscape Gardening
Orchids
Garden Construction
Herbs
Japanese Gardens
Gardening Under Lights
Greenhouse Gardening
Bulbs
Vines
Perennials
Trees
Decorating With Plants
Roses
Cacti and Succulents
Flowering House Plants
Ferns
PRETTY STORY BOOK

FOREWORD

If you have ever felt borderline crazy during the maddening process of choosing a white paint, you have come to the right book. The following pages are packed with genius tips and strategies for decorating with the nuanced, occasionally baffling color, whether your style is rustic (page 39), modern (page 119), classic (page 69), or vintage (page 87).

And because country spaces should consistently feel cozy, you'll also find plenty of ways to take the color from cold to comfortable. Throughout this book, you'll find DIY ideas (*Craft It!*), vintage shopping tips (*Collect It!*), and creative makeover projects (*Paint It!*) that add warmth, texture, and patina to neutral spaces. Don't miss the chapter on classic country combos (page 143), which showcases how fresh blue, red, yellow, and black can feel when paired with the crisp colorway.

So whether you're seeking proof that a pristine palette can be family-friendly (page 9), craving new ways to warm it up (page 30), or simply looking for a paint color you can love for posterity (page 171), we've got you covered like a cable-knit blanket.

Happy (stress-free) decorating.

Rachel Barrett

Rachel Hardage Barrett
Editor in Chief

Aurange

Chapter 1

WHY WHITE?

It's no exaggeration to say that white is the single most nimble color in the decorating arsenal. Depending on the texture and undertones, it can range from rich, warm shades to ethereal, cool hues. Whether your style is rustic, vintage, classic, or modern, white interiors can carry the aesthetic. And white, for all its purity, also has a bit of visual trickery up its sleeve. It can lighten a dim room, make a small space appear larger, obscure unsightly features, or emphasize prized ones. What's more, despite its sometimes-bad rap, white is an easier-to-maintain color choice than it may seem. (No, really!) Read on to discover hundreds of reasons to put your spaces in neutral.

WHITE IS TIMELESS

Color trends come and go. But white is here to stay. From classic Roman architecture all the way on through to sleek mid-century décor, white has been a mainstay. As such, it's a no-regrets shade used to coat walls and style furniture and accessories. It's a safe bet that it will read equal parts fresh and classic decades down the road.

The white in this sunny breakfast nook infuses it with an enduring style. What's more, the color choice ensures the space will be equally appealing for years to come.

An impressive collection of eighteenth-century English ironstone serves up a smart display. These coveted white antiques take on a graphic, almost modern air when set against a cream-hued cupboard.

From the cabinetry to the paneling, white envelops this farmhouse kitchen. The pure-as-snow color choice highlights the rustic accents while simultaneously bringing a dash of polish to the cooking space.

WHITE IS VARIED

White is not a one-note shade. Within the white spectrum there is a rainbow of iterations. If you look carefully at the undertones, some are blue or gray, others pink or yellow, and even others are green. The immense variety results in wonderfully diverse tones from stark white to ivory and tan.

From the vibrant white fabric on the sofa to the ivory backgrounds on the botanical posters and the washed-out wood dresser, this cozy California living room showcases how varying shades of white come together for a layered space.

Nearly a dozen neutral shades give this white bedroom endless depth. Decorative flourishes such as the pleated bed skirt and spindle-leg nightstands further enhance the effect.

This pass-through Texas dining room deftly showcases the diversity of white, ranging from tan walls to a gleaming white table.

WHITE IS FLEXIBLE

A room painted white provides light, tranquility, and a sense of spaciousness. And in that blank canvas, endless possibilities can bloom. Unlike so many other colors in the swatch book, white is endlessly versatile. Depending on the accessories and architecture, it can seem right at home amongst romantic, rough-hewn, and austere décor. When you change your mind and decide to embrace an aesthetic of a different flavor, white is ready and waiting to mix things up with you.

White projects cosmopolitan panache in this combined dining room and kitchen, where the crisp walls make a debonair combo with ebony furnishings and polished nickel fixtures.

White-washed metal chairs surround a farmhouse table in the kitchen of a renovated barn. A multilayered display of antique whiteware above the window reinforces the easygoing vibe.

This bedroom's white backdrop lets multiple styles—from completely country (toolbox and tobacco basket) to utterly chic (polished nickel sconces and lucite chair)—rest in perfect harmony.

WHITE IS PRACTICAL

Forget what you've heard: White isn't impossible to maintain. White fabrics are surprisingly resilient when it comes to sticky hands, panting pets, and even red wine spills. Specialty textiles such as faux leather or outdoor-grade twill can be wiped clean in an instant. And what could be easier than throwing slipscovers, bedding, and more into the washing machine for an old-fashioned bleaching? With case goods and cabinetry, chips and chinks will actually be far less noticeable on white pieces than something with a dark stain or paint job.

Yes, white works with pets! Here, white porch paint proved a smart material to coat the floors, ceiling, and walls of a potting shed. The combo of the bright hue and durable finish come together for an eye-pleasing and easy-to-scrub work area.

Paint-drop cloth curtains?
Twill slipcovers?
Cozy kid-approved hangout?
Check. Check. And
(no need to double) check.
These easy-to-wash items
create a casual family room
that lets children play and
Mom or Dad rest easy.

Have kids? Bring on the white kitchen, where spills of all varieties can be tackled with a bit of bleach and elbow grease and nuisances like scuffs and, yes, dust are more easily forgiven. This Minnesota kitchen incorporates textured surfaces such as the distressed farm table and shiplap walls to help wear and tear fly even further under the radar.

WHITE IS FORGIVING

A coat of white paint has the magic ability to hide flaws. It can raise a ceiling, open up an awkward space, and create an airy envelope in which an eclectic array of furnishings can shine. Sometimes white can obliterate architectural quirks (so long, shoddy molding) or mask unwanted elements (good-bye, exposed water pipe).

This 1748 New England cottage was crafted from a salvaged schooner. Bright white paint gives the hodgepodge of materials (brick, stucco, split rails, and more) a refresh and lets the cramped hallway feel cohesive, not chaotic.

The worn-out wood floors and past-its-prime plaster walls of this country house are pretty once again. All it took to revive them? A triple coat of white paint.

WHITE IS WELCOMING

White makes fast friends. No matter the shade or saturation, it allows all colors—from classic navy to screaming neon green—to be seen in the best possible light. It also keeps happy company with neutral cousins such as gray and taupe.

White sofas are an endlessly fun spot to play with color accents. Here, patriotic red, white, and blue details make for a folksy-meets-nautical all-American vibe.

Chartreuse walls make a bold statement in a master bathroom outfitted with a gleaming white soaking tub. A pair of diaphanous white shower curtains softens the intense paint pick.

Chapter 2

WHITE DONE RIGHT

White may technically be devoid of color, but don't think for a moment that a mostly white or ivory space has to feel sterile or laboratory-like or, for that matter, dull. There's nothing country about that after all. From mirrors to textured rugs, these little decorative accents will instantly warm up a plain white room, ensuring it has as much heart and soul as it does airy ambience.

SUBTLE PATTERNS

Want pattern without distracting from the serene vibe of a neutral space? Opt for understated designs, like the brown stripes on these club chairs, for just the right visual interest. Brown cording on the chairs and pillows provides another delicate touch.

EXPOSED BEAMS

Sure, it's easier if you live in an old colonial or tudor where they're likely lying in wait somewhere beneath the drywall. But if you reside in a new construction, don't despair! You can get the flavor with faux ones. Trust us—they can pass as real! You need only see this living room to prove it.

A MIRROR (OR TEN!)

This decorating staple will boost a space's natural light, patina, and softness, depending on its finish and shape. Here, a bevy of vintage mirrors in varying shapes and sizes make a tiny bathroom (shared by a family of five!) seem sunnier and more spacious.

SKIRTED FURNITURE

Think about it: A skirt adds more movement than stick-straight legs. From entry tables to storage benches to occasional chairs, like those shown here, skirted furniture generates ladylike flounce without veering into prissy territory.

TEXTURE UNDERFOOT

A natural-fiber rug instantly grounds a pristine white room by incorporating a woven layer. A no-fuss element, natural-fiber rugs are a smart choice for adding texture.

Fiber Rugs 101

Here's what to know about three common varieties.

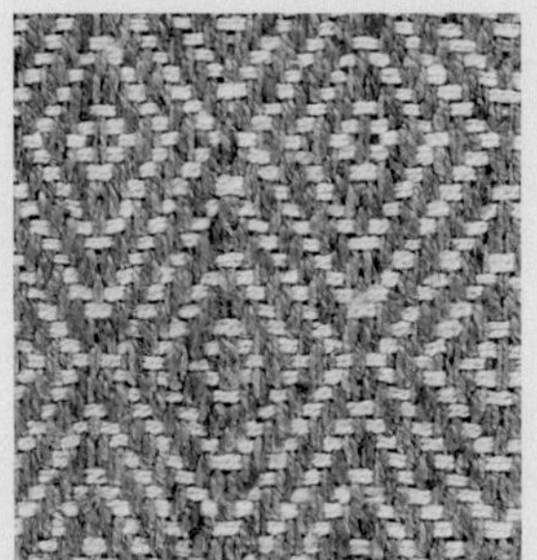

JUTE

Good for the living room thanks to a thicker, nubby weave that can handle high traffic (pets included). It's also the softest of the three.

SISAL

Good for the bedroom. It lies nice and flat and is thus better if you plan to layer softer rugs on top.

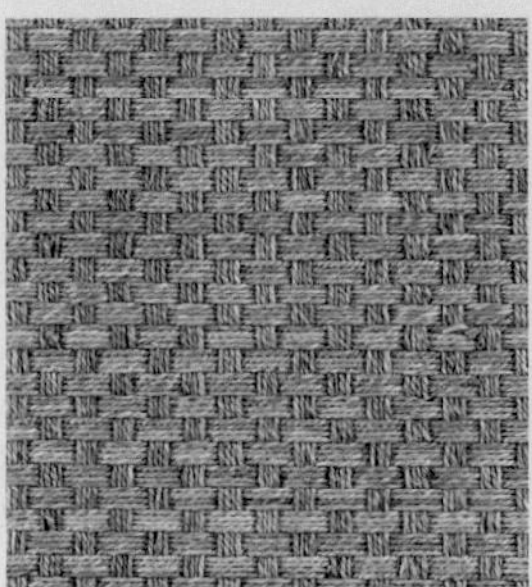

SEAGRASS

Good for the dining room, because crumbs are less likely to hide out in its supertight weave. (Take note: It's also the least barefoot friendly.)

GRAPHIC TILE

Chances are your tub, toilet, and sink are white porcelain, so skip the single-color tile in the bathroom in favor of something with a little more character. From black and white to taupe and white to something off-the-charts fun like blue and yellow, a bold design—even in a small dose—will enliven a wash space. Try tiles made from concrete or ceramic for a grittier finish and, in turn, more age-old charm.

PLANKED FLOORS

This eighteenth-century hand-hewn wood floor is especially beautiful with its perfectly imperfect, unevenly cut planks. But if you don't have the real deal at your disposal (or in your budget) you can create a similar effect with new mixed-width offerings from national floor retailers.

THROW PILLOWS

It's no surprise this cushion accent increases the sit-and-stay-awhile quotient of any room. That especially rings true when they blast color and pattern into an otherwise neutral space.

Find Your Type!

GRAPHIC

CHECKERED

FLORAL

STRIPED

POP OF BLACK

Many designers will tell you that any room looks better with a touch of black. This oversize chalkboard hits the mark in a decidedly country way. Other farmhouse-approved means to the dark side: silhouettes, cast-iron skillets, and graphite sketches.

PRETTY PLANTS

Living things boost energy in a space. Maidenhair and Boston ferns, snake plants, and herbs such as rosemary get high marks for their hardiness (Read: They're hard to kill.) and bring lushness to a bookshelf, console, or table. For something a tad daintier, try white allium.

PLEATED CURTAINS

Don't limit this gathered effect to windows as it's an equally effective way to frame beds, doorways, and bathtubs. We like a French two-pleat style (below) for a not-too-formal vibe.

OIL PAINTINGS

Rich colors and abundant textures (those brush strokes!) lend sophisticated patina to a room. Whether you favor portraits, still life, or landscapes, it's a design element worth getting hung up on.

A WARM GLOW

Lighting is a surefire way to whip up ambience. For chandeliers, skip the sleek finishes for something more organic and textured like this bedroom's statement-making driftwood fixture. Layering in task lighting, such as these bedside sconces, will also enhance the warmth.

LAYERS. LAYERS. AND MORE LAYERS.

Rely on irresistible textures, such as thick wool, raw linen, and gleaming ceramics to fill an otherwise cold space. These layers of tactile items are begging to be touched.

SOMETHING OLD

As these steamer-trunks-turned-nightstands perfectly illustrate, nothing zaps that stark feeling faster than weathered antiques.

OPEN SHELVING

A hallmark of country kitchens, this everything-in-plain-sight strategy helps a space feel more collected and, as a result, more cozy.

BRASS HARDWARE

It's easy to see why this gold-like metal is having a design moment. It's warmer than glass or bronze and won't showcase fingerprints like polished nickel often does. Try it on plumbing fittings (below), cabinet hardware, lighting, and more.

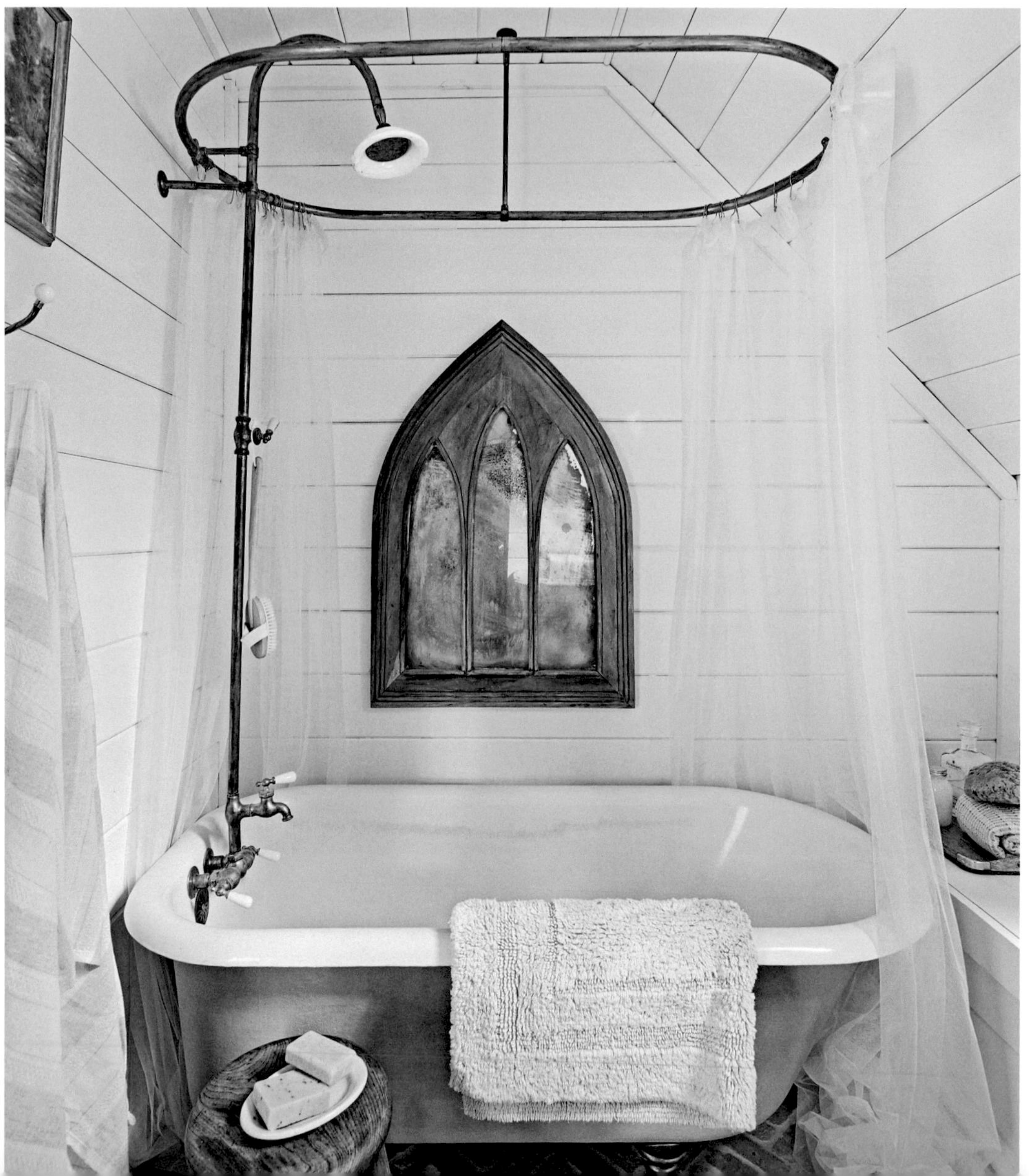

MIXED FINISHES

Look closely: This (mostly) white kitchen is rich and layered thanks to a broad mix of materials, from wood and marble countertops to bronze and brass hardware to painted and natural wood floors. The cohesive blend offsets the potential frigidity of the sleek stainless-steel hood and appliances.

NOT-NEUTRAL "NEUTRALS"

That's right: Certain light paint colors can act as neutrals. If you crave a hint of color, try paint with a dash of another hue included in the paint formula. This nearly white kitchen, for example, incorporates light pink floors and pale gray cabinetry for a nuanced take on the neutral kitchen.

SHAPELY SILHOUETTES

Form takes center stage when using a predominately white color palette that's free from distracting bright colors and patterns. The eye goes straight toward powerful shapes first—the bold lines of a lamp or vase (above), or the particular curve of a table leg or chair back.

Entertaining
HOME

Chapter 3

RUSTIC WHITE

Despite its pristine qualities, white is far from austere. In fact, it makes a practically magical pairing with rustic interiors. It can immediately cure cabin fever in even the most abundantly wood-clad rooms. A generous dose of white (and its cousins cream and ivory) immediately brightens a rough-hewn area, infusing it with a degree of lightness. From furnishings (both painted and upholstered) and pale-hued collectibles to a good ol' wash on paneled walls, white is often just the breath of fresh air a rustic space needs to feel complete.

Conversely, an all-white interior can be warmed up by rustic accents. A dash of exposed wood posts or unpainted moldings can take a room from cold to cozy. Beyond architectural elements, decorative accents such as barnwood shelving, chipping furniture, and nature-inspired light fixtures are sure to take the edge off a buttoned-up neutral space.

BENCH MARK

A vintage bench with a worn finish and a pair of weathered pillows are the only furnishings needed in the hallway of this 160-year-old farmhouse, where a similarly rustic ladder leads to a quaint sleeping loft.

NATURAL SELECTION

Nature can provide the perfect pale accessories in a white interior. Here, sun-blanched seashells rest atop a chest built from weathered scrap lumber.

BUILT FOR BUSINESS

A fresh coat of white paint transforms this once horse stable to a farmhouse kitchen. Now a handsome and hardworking space, the decor features reclaimed wood, antique furnishing, and vintage finds.

LEATHER WEATHER

Brown leather may seem ho-hum, but don't underestimate its ability to play nice with a white room. Here, a worn-in mahogany leather rocker adds visual depth and a come-sit-and-stay-awhile air to the neutral bedroom.

KNOTTY AND NICE

White stain allows the knotty pine to show through on the walls and ceiling in this 1850s farmhouse, taking the edge off the massive post and beams. The coffee table—old boards affixed to a chicken crate—repeats the frame's hue.

MATERIAL WORLD

Texture reigns in this Tennessee cabin kitchen. Countertops crafted from a single piece of white oak, sink supports upcycled from old wood columns, and a show-stopping ceiling inlaid with hundreds of pieces of barnwood bring interest to the white cooking space. Chippy white factory lights finish out the patinaed style.

CABIN IN THE WOODS

Bright white is the ideal shade with which to coat this lake cabin's exposed wall planks and beams—highlighting the imperfections and helping the small space to feel larger. The room is also impervious to dampness thanks to a durable wicker sectional covered in indoor/outdoor upholstery.

BETTER WITH AGE

The genius of this compact New England kitchen? It will only appear more striking in years to come. From the reclaimed wood cabinets to the sheet metal countertops and soapstone sink—even the unlacquered brass hardware—these elements are designed to take wear and tear and acquire patina over time.

Collect It!

Green glassware can be snatched up for mere pennies and lends a verdant pop to a cook space.

MIRROR, MIRROR

An old mirror proves an intriguing backdrop to a collection of tiny white creamers that sit on a honey-hued dresser. The mirror's driftwood frame and pearly surface help to ground the petite assortment, which would otherwise be lost and out of scale against blank white walls.

ROLL WITH IT

A vintage baker's rack serves as a beautiful venue to store dishware. The exposed framework offers ample texture and interest to the plain room, without erring on overly decorated.

Bright Idea

Keep kitchen wares in plain sight for storage-cum-art installation with utilitarian panache.

CABINET MEMBERS

Because they are all white, these mismatched porcelain pieces read as a set. Plus the collection pops against the chipping greens and blues of the nineteenth-century cabinet.

PERFECT TIN

Textured accents don't have to equal rough-hewn wood. (Though those are certainly welcome!) In this kitchen, the homeowner complemented the raised finishes of the shiplap walls and hammered zinc sink with a pressed tin ceiling painted a steely shade of charcoal gray.

ISLAND TIME

Handsome kitchen islands can add the right touch of rusticity to a pretty but nondescript neutral kitchen. This green desk, which the homeowner scored for $350 at an antiques shop in Mexico, now creates a one-of-a-kind work station. To further the functionality (and texture!), the homeowner improvised a lower shelf by propping wood boards atop the stretchers.

Collect It!

Vintage vegetable crates are versatile and far more eye pleasing than standard plastic storage bins.

INTO THE WOODS

This kitchen, with its painted white cabinets and walls and a charming 1950s refrigerator, feels anything but spare by embracing an array of organic textures: lush green foliage in a galvanized tin, homemade tree-trunk stools, and an old farm table.

BRANCHING OUT

A clean coat of white paint unifies the disparate materials and textures found in the kitchen of this Cape Cod–style home—including a statement-making tree-turned-vertical beam.

CITY SAVVY

This tiny New York dwelling oozes country flair with rough-hewn collectibles set against neutral walls and mirrors. In the dining room the homeowner's display-it-don't-store-it philosophy is showcased with linens lining an old orchard ladder.

THE MORE THE MERRIER

Weathered collectibles (duck decoys, antique cloches, and old suitcases, to name a few) stave off dullness in this rustic but somewhat plain Texas dining room. Accenting the organic quality of the accessories are a cluster of potted herbs and a vaseful of cheery yellow tulips.

Craft It!

Fashion a graphic table runner using black-and-white fabric cut to fit the table (most will require about three yards) and "hemmed" along the edges with a no-sew adhesive.

IN THE WASH

White and rustic become one on the dining room walls of a 135-year-old cabin on Washington's Vashon Island. The homeowner treated the room's original paneling with a soft wash that plays up the perfectly imperfect irregularities of the century-old wood.

Collect It!

American flags produce an instant sense of place in a room. Search for older versions with fewer than fifty stars for a truly unique buy.

LOOKING UP

Believe it or not, this character-filled dining room is located in an old military barrack. The rugged aesthetic was achieved with plenty of white paint and a bevy of natural elements: pine farm table, unfinished benches, antique hickory chairs, flax curtains, and a rattan plant stand. But the crowning achievement is, of course, the bird's nest–esque chandelier handmade from broken hickory twigs.

LESS IS MORE

A sense of simplicity infuses an Upstate New York home with spare white walls. The living-dining area is decorated with a mix of wood furnishings, including Indonesian rush-back loungers and an antique American farm table with cane-seat chairs.

WALK THE PLANKS

The owners of this upstate New York farmhouse undertook an ambitious DIY project, adorning the ceiling, walls, and floors of a previously unfinished space with white wood paneling. The "new" look feels right at home with the house's primitive vernacular. A stately taxidermy, rescued from a now-closed Brooklyn boutique, pulls the great outdoors into the sleeping quarters.

Bright Idea

For a balanced design, place beadboard panels on walls and ceiling in opposite directions.

BARN AND BRED

A statement-making rough-hewn headboard pours country charm into an all-white bedroom. The rustic (and affordable!) piece was made to replicate barn doors from reclaimed shipping pallets sanded and stained with a soft white-gray for a welcoming, weathered look.

Craft It!

To create a barn door headboard, affix two-by-four boards to a framework slightly wider than your mattress. Then affix two additional boards overtop for X-brace detailing. The finished product belies its easy construction!

Collect It!

Paint-by-numbers have a textured appeal that sits well with white surroundings. *Bonus:* Many can be had for less than $10.

TWICE AS NICE

The twiggy Adirondack beds in this kids' room are outfitted in classic country style with white coverlets, striped wool trading blankets, and old-fashioned plaid pillows, and provide a tidy contrast to the bright collection of vintage paintings clustered above. Distressed white frames unify and elevate the thrift store artwork collection.

BATHING BEAUTY

This rough-hewn space seamlessly combines a bedroom and bathroom. Its serene vibe comes from a contrast in textures and whites, including gleaming porcelain, weathered wood and iron, soft linens, and fresh flowers.

PANEL DISCUSSION

Sunshine streams in through a tall (bare!) window, bouncing light off a bed completely covered in nubby white linen. Set in an envelope of walls, ceiling, and floor clad in burnished planks, the effect is warm and comforting.

IRONING IT OUT

An iron bed frame offers a delicate counterpoint to this studio bedroom's hefty beams and uprights. What's more, it softens the peninsula effect of the white bed against the dark wood and floors.

SINK SIMPLICITY

This refreshingly rustic bathroom keeps things simple—a no-frills vanity crafted from fir, toiletries decanted in glass containers, and white towels stored in a basket below.

Craft It!

Adjoin two side tables with a sink base made from two-by-four boards. Paint or stain all the same finish for a cohesive final product.

PEAK PERFORMANCE

A once-awkward, steeply pitched bathroom is now a focal point thanks to a rustic accent wall. Made of two-inch thick wood slices glued to a plywood backing, the mosaic mimics the appearance of stacked firewood, producing a warm contrast to the rest of the room's white walls.

Bright Idea

In lieu of windows, a pair of skylights bathes this space with flattering light from above.

Chapter 4

CLASSIC WHITE

Thanks to its versatility, white is the ultimate classic shade. Which is why a neutral palette, all-American motifs, and old-fashioned antiques are the hallmarks of classic country style. These elements make for a timeless look and also pack surprising versatility that can skew luxurious or laid back, depending on your preference. Traditional furnishings and dressmaker details, for example, will yield sophistication, while the look is just as easily dressed down with loose slipcovers, subtle patterns, and natural materials. Regardless of what direction you choose, this tailored take on white has plenty of room for layering in your own personality and mixing it up over time.

STAIR IN THE FACE

Nuance is essential to staving off boredom in a classic white room. Here, varying shades and saturations of taupe-tinged white yield depth in the largely monochromatic entryway. Adding to that depth are stair risers wallpapered in a sharp trellis pattern.

OUT ON A LEDGE

Casual furnishings outfitted in an array of white shades and a subtle range of pale hues on the walls, ceiling, and trim create a dreamy backdrop for this all-white collection of American Art Pottery.

Bright Idea

When displaying a monochromatic collection, arrange similar objects together so the repeated shapes will have the most impact.

BASKET CASE

A classic basket weave pattern on the tile backsplash brings graphic whimsy to the country kitchen, which features cast-iron cabinet hardware and an extra-wide apron front sink.

Craft It!

The squared-off edges of scrap plywood make for petite corner shelving, just right for displaying pint-size collectibles.

PEEKABOO PIECES

This family room is a beautiful example of how a subtle variety of white shades, textures, and shapes can breathe life into a classic neutral space. The standout of the room: a collection of white ironstone china lining the built-in shelves that look through to the equally airy kitchen.

UPON REFLECTION

Nothing catches the eye quite like the twinkling combination of mirrors and glass. Here, a collection of glass bottles used as bud vases lines a white mantel, while the mirror doubles the visual impact of both the flowers and the light. Sprigs of native grasses can be just as chic as costly florist blooms.

Collect It!

Silhouettes can be found by the basketful at most flea markets. Expect ones bearing an entire scene (as opposed to just a profile) to carry a higher price tag.

PROFILE PICS

Pops of black liven up a classic, neutral space. Here, a duo of oval-framed childhood silhouette portraits creates a focal point in this white, shiplap-lined cooking space.

MINT CONDITION

A classic white country kitchen makes a seamless spot to showcase a prized collection, such as the green dishware abundantly displayed here.

Collect It!

Jadeite, an opaque green glassware originally used in 1940s diners, is a versatile collectible that mixes well with neutral décor.

CALIFORNIA DREAMING

With its white walls and terracotta floors this country kitchen presents a California twist on the traditional. The warmth established from the flooring is carried through to rustic accents, including the farmhouse table used in place of a traditional island.

GOOD FORM

Black antique brass fixtures and a twiggy wood table cut striking silhouettes in this airy breakfast room.

HIGHS AND LOWS

This sun-filled dining space piles on texture from the paneled ceiling to the linen curtain panels right on down to the rustic table and patterned seat cushions.

Collect It!

Demijohn bottles are characterized by their round shape and short necks. Spring for green ones to add a verdant pop of color.

Collect It!

Books with similarly colored spines lend an artful touch to a room, whether casually displayed in a pile or more formally lining a shelf.

LADY IN WAITING

This serene bedroom is the very picture of country refinement. Railroad trestle beams add heft and contrast overhead, while a commanding flea-market oil portrait watches over the antique bed.

GRAY OUT

Subtle color accents also mix well with white. Here, a handsome silver-gray throw on a linen-upholstered bed picks up the cast of a Venetian cut-glass mirror from the 1920s.

DIAMOND IN THE (NOT-SO) ROUGH

This white tub alcove gets its personality from contrasting shapes—the round lip of the bathtub against the straight lines of the built-in ledge and the crisscross design of the original diamond grid windows. Contrast also appears in the form of dark hues such as the sculptural wood vase, assorted picture frames, and stool in the largely white canvas.

AWASH IN STYLE

Passed down from the homeowner's grandmother, the mahogany china cabinet makes a striking, unexpected statement. So much so that it *almost* overshadows the beautiful cast-iron clawfoot tub. An antique rug helps to warm up a neutral, utilitarian space.

BEDROOM BLUES

This Tennessee bedroom may have hints of blue, but it still reads as a neutral space with its focus on texture and pattern over vibrancy.

NICKELS AND PENNIES

Gleaming materials, such as high-gloss penny tile floors and polished nickel plumbing fixtures, create an inviting bathroom that feels at one with its lush surroundings.

US
66
JANELLE TAYLOR · FOLLOW THE WIND

Chapter 5

VINTAGE WHITE

For many a country house—set against idyllic pastoral scenery—is the ultimate restorative escape. But even with less scenic views, soft layered rooms in the midst of a suburban or city dwelling can have the same transformative power, taking on the sense of a retreat. Plenty of weather-worn and old pieces can imbue a space with a feeling that it's a world away from modern noise and frenzy. From bedrooms piled with quilts to shelves chock-full of collections, vintage white spaces are best served with a heaping helping of patina.

TRIPLE THREAT

This farmhouse fireplace presents a trio of vintage flair with two old signs and framed photo strips topping the mantel display.

Paint It!

Coating a brick fireplace in the same shade as the wall generates visual respite in a small room.

IN BLOOM

A wall of thrift store floral paintings (featuring many faded iterations of pink and yellow) anchor the towering ceilings of a white living room. What's more, the affordable artwork balances the off-center window.

Craft It!

This coffee table is simply a dining table with the legs cut down to accommodate the scale of the sofa and chairs.

PLATTER UP

The vintage white aesthetic can also extend to the tabletop. Here, an impressive assortment of ironstone brings some dignified visual heft to a farm table.

OPEN DOOR POLICY

Architectural elements can also generate vintage style in a neutral room. In this otherwise forgettable corner, an antique door (with its original mint paint job and hand-lettered signage) creates a lively focal point with a past of its own.

CARRY A TORCH

In lieu of standard lighting, the homeowner opted for reproduction lanterns equipped with battery-operated candles. At three and a half feet tall, they make an impressive statement without overpowering the small, neutral sitting room.

SCALE UP

This small living room lives large with—surprise!—several oversize vintage pieces including a nine-foot-long French sofa and a beefy wingback chair. The neutral items artfully blend with their surroundings, making them well-suited instead of overpowering.

LOST AND FOUND

This deconstructed gallery wall showcases a quirky assortment of found white (with dashes of black) objects the homeowner has accumulated over the years and deemed too pretty to throw away. Among the pieces are sentimental items (her grandmother's sunglasses and husband's prize 4-H ribbon) and random castoffs (paint brush, playing card, and scissors).

GENERAL (STORE) RULE

This salvaged general-store-refrigerator-turned-pantry features beautifully preserved signage and hundreds of scuffs and scratches. The homeowner simply topped the shelving with a clear coat of polyurethane to make it dry-goods ready.

IN TUNE

A dark-wood piano was striking a jarring chord among the neutral décor of a Montana home. That is until the homeowner coated it in an ivory chalk paint, giving it a matte finish in keeping with both its age and surroundings.

CLIMB THE WALLS

A weathered china cabinet (filled with a hodgepodge of antique earthenware) pairs perfectly with an antique wallpaper featuring a climbing vine motif. The soft colors of the wall covering echo the faded lines of the hutch.

GARAGE SALE

An antiques-loving homeowner topped an auto garage storage console with gray-veined marble for truly custom cabinetry oozing with character. (Originally painted a bold blue, she stripped down the raw wood for a less industrial look.) The chippy workbench-turned-island gives a cool hint of color.

Paint It!

Hardwoods don't have to be stained. Here, marine paint provides the kitchen's rustic elements with a gleaming counterpoint.

CUT A RUG

This classic farmhouse kitchen, complete with a beadboard backsplash and distressed island, generates interest underfoot with a patterned outdoor rug cut to fit the size of the room. The eye-catching design was also a practical one—no grout lines to keep clean.

THROWING SHADE

Shades like white, khaki, and light blue create the illusion of space (a particularly welcome touch in cramped guest quarters). Peppering a few patterns into the scheme, like that found on the bedding, increases the visual depth.

LET IT BE

When a homeowner came across this clawfoot tub, she went with her gut and left the copper-tinged exterior as is. It's a refined hue in the neutral bathroom and, in fact, inspired the colorway on the striped curtain panels.

EAVES DROPPING

In an all-white room, corners can easily become visual craters. Enter a handsome assortment of vintage finds. Here, an antique painter's tray, mounted antlers, a 1930s company photo, and iron-stone pieces bring personality to an otherwise unused spot in a bathroom.

TUB TIME

This spiffy white bathroom is anything but sterile with the addition of an antique trough sink. The farmhouse find features a zinc finish that has acquired a handsome grittiness over time.

SMOOTH SAILING

A neutral space need not be boring! Sometimes all it takes to rev an all-white kitchen is one or two unexpected vintage accents. In this Hamptons example, a sailboat model and a trio of salvaged ship lights help cook up character.

Bright Idea

The tiles' concave center and milky-white glaze add an old-world texture that stands out against the sleek new appliances.

CARVING STATION

It's not the blush coverlet that ushers interest into this neutral bedroom. Instead, intricate carvings on the antique headboard, mirror, and side tables pepper the area with depth and they-don't-make-'em-like-they-used-to style.

Bright Idea

A salvaged window frame filters the light without fussy window treatments.

SKIRT THE ISSUE

Rather than install traditional lower cabinets, the homeowner used a plywood framework fronted with fabric to stylishly conceal utilitarian pots and pans. The nubby burlap incorporates a rough-hewn texture to the whimsical white kitchen.

ZINC ABOUT IT

A handful of zinc fixtures—some rusted-out, some still with a bit of shine—gives the utilitarian space a vintage vibe.

CHECKS AND BALANCES

A bevy of worn furniture instantly puts you at ease in this pretty and inviting dining room. Adding to the comfortable aesthetic are floor-to-ceiling buffalo check curtains. Though new, they mimic the softness of the vintage pieces.

TABLE MATTERS

This dining table proves a showstopper thanks to its massive circa-1800s corbel base and pale blue shutter top. Covered with a sheet of glass (cut with smooth, rounded edges) the combo anchors this eating area with memorable, one-of-a-kind style.

Craft It!

Give your own table this charming spoon holder detail by using a Dremel® tool to create notches along one end.

CHIPPING IN

What makes this no-frills table and bench a stunner? The wonderfully worn-out paint jobs. Letting paint peel and fleck in its own due course brings a richness to a room that's hard to match.

Bright Idea

A graphic vintage hotel sign draws attention away from the hardworking heat and air wall unit above.

SHAPELY SIGHTS

Form is an integral element when using a predominately white color palette. In this sunny dining nook, a curvaceous chair commands attention.

BRIGHT EXPECTATIONS

A vintage white aesthetic can embrace bright white. Here, it's shown on both the centuries-old woodwork and the antique iron bed. A stately oil painting and tarnished silver lamp infuse the small space with well-suited finish.

AT FIRST BLUSH

A pink (yes, pink!) marble remnant is the right dash of personality for this kitchen coffee station. It's soft ivory veining pairs well with the cupboard's chippy paint and French pottery.

KEEP POSTED

This under-the-eaves bedroom embraces the existing architecture by placing the old wrought iron bed (painted a barely there shade of blue) in front of not one but two windows and also behind a support post. The unexpected positioning is right at home among the weatherworn items.

Craft It!

These stunning "hardwoods" were created from sheets of plywood cut down to wide planks and stained a soft gray wash that pairs well with the all-white interior.

TRIPLE THREAT

Distressed finishes (old street signs, side tables, and storage trunks) lend a relaxed feel to this no-frills bunkroom. Antique iron beds and sconces add to the casualness.

Paint It!

Replicate the look of an industrial shipping crate by stenciling numbers onto a store-bought replica.

SIGN OF THE TIMES

Vintage signage infuses a newly refurbished neutral space with plenty of old soul. This eye-catching ANTIQUES sign incorporates storied style that's matched by the chipping paint of the mirror below.

Collect It!

Antique French pantry containers make especially romantic vessels for decanting soaps and bath salts.

LET IN THE LIGHT

A yard of cheesecloth strewn from shaker pegs above the window creates privacy without blocking precious natural light. The gauzy fabric also complements the tub with a soft, feminine finish.

Chapter 6

MODERN WHITE

Clean, crisp rooms are the modern standard bearer. This look may seem at odds with a country aesthetic, which is more often than not dominated by collections and heavy doses of patina. But the fact of the matter is that nothing frames a country view quite like a dazzling all-white space. A simple palette and minimalist lines create a fresh and calming atmosphere where nature can take center stage. What's more, a monochromatic room offers unique opportunities to experiment with rich textures and eclectic accessories. Last but not least, there are many times that a mod pop of white is just the graphic touch a rustic room needs for a dash of visual reprieve.

WALK THE LINE

Interspersed vertical and horizontal lines give this farmhouse a modern angle, so to speak. The varying directions (horizontal-planked walls, vertical-paneled doors) pile on graphic panache.

Craft It!

This door's panels are accented with dark blue paper tape.

LIGHT WORKLOAD

Beautiful black-and-white photographs casually displayed with pushpins and binder clips yield a certain effortless glamour. A stack of coffee-table books reinforces the low-key perfection.

Craft It!

On non-load-bearing ceilings you can install copycat beams made from medium-density fiberboard–wrapped Styrofoam. (*Tip:* Tape off your desired orientation before adhering to ensure a proper fit.)

BEAM ME UP

A modern look can still have plenty of wooden qualities. The trick is texture and saturation. Here, smooth birch beams adorn the ceiling of a neutral entryway, bringing clean lines and warm tones.

Collect It!

Cloches—glassed domes intended for forcing outdoor plants indoors—make for an endlessly versatile collector's item, with pretty curves and a showcasing effect for vignettes.

HAND-ME-DOWNS

Antiques can feel au courant when presented in a deconstructed and monochromatic scheme. Here, the curves of the glass cloche, mannequin hand, and feathers are decidedly avant-garde alongside the white walls.

FARMHOUSE 2.0

A family room in a 1930s Connecticut farmhouse was feeling gray and dated. Enter a white paint job and flush-mounted sandstone hearth. The new façades are in keeping with the country locale, but also provide a crisp backdrop for showcasing industrial pieces like the steel-framed sofa.

TITANS OF INDUSTRY

A neutral backdrop of white paneled walls and wood planked floors makes for a smart contrast to the manufacturing-grade elements found throughout this living room, including the wire stair railings and pipe-fitting light fixture.

Craft It!

These railings are simply rolls of thick-gauge chicken wire affixed directly to the bannister.

FRESH START

New white paint highlights the historic architecture of this California bungalow. It also makes an airy anchor for the homeowner to layer Bohemian accents.

Paint It!

A hodgepodge of thrift-store picture frames appear instantly cohesive when coated with black paint.

GRAPHIC MATERIAL

An old black-and-white train sign provides a strong focus to a creamy white wall hung with a jumble of prints framed in unifying black. A factory stool and bare floor reinforce the less-is-more look.

WATCH THE CLOCK

Sometimes all it takes to give a room a modern air is one graphic white accent. Here, a laser-cut cuckoo clock packs that punch, striking a hip chord in the otherwise traditional setting.

Paint It!

You can achieve a similar style by swathing a vintage cuckoo clock in white paint. (Be sure to open and close the bird's door several times while drying, as to prevent it from getting stuck in one position.)

TO THE LETTER

White pottery in a wealth of shapes is set against a similarly white wall to give this sitting room tone-on-tone depth and texture. A few strategic hits of black—including the ebony *Y*—break up the vignette with graphic aplomb.

Craft It!

Give a bookshelf an instant facelift by replacing standard-issue book jackets with matching white ones cut from vellum or craft paper.

SHELF LIFE

Modern and monochromatic go hand in hand. Here, a soothing white theme unifies an eclectic assortment of old and new cameras, ceramics, bottles, and books. The latter are used as risers to incorporate height and interest in the vignette.

Bright Idea

A steel pot rack conserves space and also produces a utilitarian aesthetic.

STEEL THE SHOW

Sleek stainless steel and gleaming Carrara marble look snazzy in this cutting-edge chef's kitchen. The simple, everything-in-plain-sight style makes it easy to pop color by way of cookware, such as the orange pans and turquoise bowls.

HORSING AROUND

This clean living room invites with heaps of organic texture (woven baskets and potted plants) and a few rough-hewn accents (the coffee table and credenza). Pulling off the ultimate country finish is the six-foot-wide filly crafted from barnwood.

ON VIEW

Part of the reason this layered living room feels fresh and modern? It's embracing of the outdoors with expansive windows and minimal window treatments. Adding to that cocoon-feel are textured furnishings such as the rattan chair, weathered coffee table, and nubby area rug.

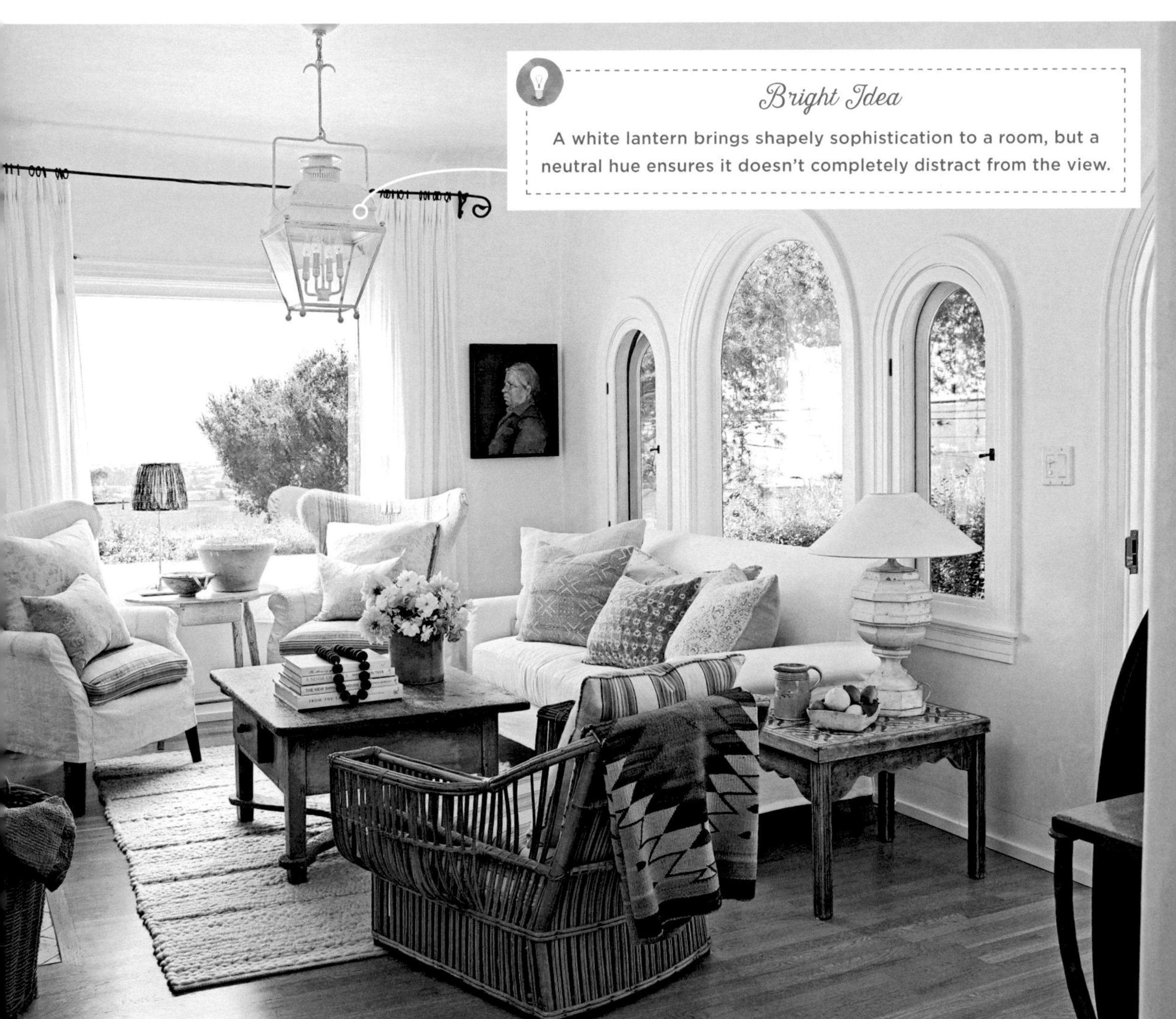

Bright Idea

A white lantern brings shapely sophistication to a room, but a neutral hue ensures it doesn't completely distract from the view.

UPPER CRUST

A kitchen with modular lower cabinetry (and no uppers!) looks fresh and feels spacious. The expanse of wall along the windows receives some visual interest with an on-trend EAT YOUR GREENS poster and assortment of shapely cutting boards.

Craft It!

The luxe effect of wraparound drapery hardware can be reproduced with pipe fittings.

SIMPLE LIFE

Simplicity is the star in this Georgia dining room. The homeowner opted for understated curtain panels and bentwood chairs to keep the focus on the stunning view. (The windows overlook a horse pasture!) A spindly tree further connects the indoors and out.

COLOR CONNECTION

Sure this kitchen has a farmhouse door. But it also produces a country effect thanks to the stark contrast between the bright white millwork and ebony-stained floors. Plus, a rainbow of barstools lends a playful finish.

Paint It!

Copy these barstools by topping off old metal ones with different shades of spray paint. (*Tip*: It's okay if the stool shapes and styles aren't an exact match.)

BLANK CANVAS

The minimalist backdrop (white walls, millwork, sink, and floors) of this apartment dining area is a perfect partner for a select assortment of brown-and-white furnishings and accessories. The ticking stripe wingbacks bring warmth to the overall austere space.

Paint It!

Tired hardwoods (or linoleum for that matter) are instantly revived with a coat of white paint. (*Tip*: Use a marine-quality option for a durable, water-resistant finish.)

STAYING AFLOAT

In a textbook example of "make the most of what you've got," homeowners converted a storage unit into cozy guest quarters. Minimalist details such as the floating side tables and single-bulb pendant allow the small space to live larger than it is.

Craft It!

These "night stands" were fabricated from wood scraps and then adhered directly to the wall with load-bearing screws.

VANITY PLATE

The star of this country bathroom is a barn door. Power-washed and repurposed as a vanity top, it is complete with two cast-iron sinks. Single-bulb light fixtures and a black pipe base give the bucolic bath a rugged vibe. A floating vanity, like this one, offers abundant, unobstructed storage below.

Collect It!

Whether you love fashion or travel or something far more irreverent, old advertisements pass as fine artwork when displayed en masse.

ON THE SCENT

This beach house bathroom is awash in white paint, raising the eave that slopes above the clawfoot tub. A chic display of pop art (vintage Chanel No. 5 magazine ads) creates interest on what could easily be an overlooked stretch of wall.

Collect It!

Vintage hat boxes invoke storied style in any space. *Bonus*: They pack in storage wherever you place them and act as a surface-like side table here.

ONE-HIT WONDER

This spacious bedroom may be located in a centuries-old barn, but it feels decidedly modern due to its enormous city loft–like windows. (They measure five by five feet!) Another contemporary twist? The single stained stripe amongst the painted white wall planks.

Chapter 7

COUNTRY COMBOS

Yes, white plays nice with every color of the rainbow. But there are certain hues for which it has a special affinity. Blue and white has universal appeal which dates back to ancient Persia; black and white are visual proof that opposites attract; red and white recalls a time when these were the most affordable paint colors to acquire in a rural setting. Today, these three pairings continue to be decorating go-tos. And for good reason. They walk the practically impossible line of evoking a classic country aesthetic that's simultaneously fresh. Here's to shade soul mates.

Blue and White

From Chinese ginger jars to Indian textiles, blue and white is steeped in universal and ancient appeal. Furthermore, a blue-and-white palette can be deployed to a widely differing effect in any number of combinations and saturations—from watery light blue and periwinkle to cobalt and navy—through paint, fabric, flooring, and collections. Deep, dark blue gives gravity to a room and, depending on the shade of its white partner, can impart a formal or casual air. Pale, whispering blues suggest simplicity and serenity, making it ideal to create a calm, restful space.

ROLE REVERSAL

This homeowner opted for a charming switch of a popular scheme—white cabinets and blue walls. Instead, a soft blue-gray adorns the cabinetry and island, while white paint coats the walls. Cool, toned gray marble countertops bridge the gap between the two.

MINT TO BE

A minty-blue wall showcases this collection of white vases to beautiful effect, while the curvaceous blue hardwood side tables provide an additional pop of color.

Collect It!

Blue-and-white china is abundantly available at most every flea market. Mix restaurant-grade pieces with true antiques for a robust grouping that doesn't break the bank.

DISH OUT

A high-low mix of cobalt ceramics—some fine antiques, some big box store buys—in a variety of patterns creates an effortless display that turns standard dishware storage into a work of art.

INTO THE BLUE

Blue-and-white china takes on new meaning in this glossy cupboard showcasing an enviable collection of white earthenware. The paint job was inspired by the circa-1700s wainscoting (shown at left) unearthed during a recent kitchen renovation.

QUILT TO LAST

Centuries-old quilts in pinwheel (left) and bear's paw (right) patterns dress these antique wrought iron beds, the differing motifs linked by their common blue-and-white scheme. A handwoven rug in similar tones adds folksy texture underfoot.

SCREEN TIME

A classic blue-and-white quilt (featuring the diamond field pattern) was used to upholster a privacy screen. The vintage piece gets a modern slant with its displayed-on-the-diagonal orientation.

DOOR JAM

A plain-Jane pantry goes country by swapping out the builder-grade door with an unexpected screened one. A blue-green paint job—similar to that found on Southern porch ceilings—strengthens the homey appeal.

BLUE STREAK

Checks, stripes, squiggles—this country bedroom packs them all in. Sticking to one color, a pretty cornflower blue, backed up by plenty of white across the varying textiles prevents chaos from setting in. Rustic accents like the pine dresser and horse silhouette also provide an eye-pleasing visual break.

CHECKMATE

Thanks to its easy-on-the-eyes appeal, blue-and-white is a color combo that lets you go big. How big? This room boasts an oversize blue-and-white gingham floor motif applied using a stencil and three shades of paint—two blue and one white.

Red and White

Quilts. Spatterware. Even many barns. Red and white is a quintessentially pastoral color pairing. In eighteenth- and nineteenth-century America, red pigments and dyes were often more affordable options—making them a logical choice for farmers, settlers, and the like. (Not to mention it was particularly eye-catching.) Today, red may not cost any less, but when paired with white, it generates legitimate country cred. Depending on the shade and finish, it can envelop a room with all-American style, retro charm, or full-blown drama—and is certain to bring an energizing quality to the space.

RETROGRADE

This happy kitchen has a retro vibe due to many hits of red—the range, hood, and the cabinet knobs. Stealing the show are sweet café curtains crafted from 1950s cotton napkins.

Craft It!

Bright napkins make sweet cafe curtains when hemmed and clipped to a simple extension rod.

SKIRT ALERT

Refusing to equate a tattered quilt with out of commission, a crafty homeowner created a skirted console table out of a beloved red-and-white coverlet featuring the rolling star pattern. The project was topped with a stained piece of plywood for a sturdy and rustic finish.

FOR THE BIRDS

This built-in entryway's fiery color was inspired by a similar shade found on the bird-filled wallpaper. Designed to resemble a piece of furniture, it's more charming than a standard closet.

IN THE RED

Red unifies a hodgepodge of elements in this cabin bedroom including numerous textile motifs and (look closely!) mismatched twin beds. Coated a glossy red, the beds have a cohesive style with just the right amount of country quirk.

BED OF ROSES

Rustic shiplap walls are the perfect foil to a sweet red-and-white color scheme in a compact Texas bedroom. The coverlet's floral motif enhances the fresh, feminine feel.

WITH THE GRAIN

Once an agrarian necessity (stripe widths let farmers differentiate their crop bags) grain sack stripes are now a bona fide country decorating motif. What's more, if you don't have a genuine antique, the red-and-white motif can be easily recreated. The table shown here was created by painting stripes down the length of the white piece. Fine grained sandpaper was rubbed along the edges of the stripes for a more rustic finish.

27

Black & White

It's a well-kept decorators' secret that every room looks better with a pop of black. And that's especially true in spaces awash in white, where the color has a grounding quality. It can instill a sophistication that feels at home among the antiques and patina found in a country setting. Meanwhile, going all in with a black and white palette creates a crispness that is unparalleled. The bold combination is timeless and transformative; the truth may be rarely black and white, but when it comes to interiors there's no debating the infallibility of the pairing.

PATTERN PLAY

From the shimmering floral wallpaper to the striped table runners, this dining room's punches of pattern make the high-contrast look a feast—not a strain—for the eyes.

SHAPE UP

Walls and trim painted high-gloss ebony throw the white shapes of the 1950s furniture into sharp relief in this hip but cozy living room.

FABRIC HOUSE

Black-and-white-striped upholstered walls (the fabric is also carried through to the window treatments) create a graphic backdrop against this two-toned room. The golden warmth of the paintings and wood dresser offset the intensity.

PRIZED POSSESSIONS

The crisp combination of charcoal black and bright white in the entryway provides the equestrian-loving homeowner a setting that anchors this collection of paintings, photos, and ribbons. Different textures—wainscoting, velvet, brass—soften the space.

Craft It!

Transform your own walls by affixing newspapers (or any other paper for that matter) with wallpaper paste and a flat sealant.

OLD NEWS

A stack of 1960s Ukrainian newspapers scored at a flea market lend quirky panache to the walls and ceiling of a small bathroom.

TRAY CHIC

An assortment of toleware trays (a style of hand-painted tin popular in the eighteenth century) provides a grounding element to the white walls and light-wood floors of a Connecticut cottage.

SMALL WONDER

Graphic black and white may seem like a no-go in spaces sparse on square footage. Not so! The trick is to pick pieces where black and white work alongside each other. Here, the striped rug, inlay dresser, and antique oil portraits put the combo into singular pieces, as opposed to high-contrast color-block elements.

WGW35
WGW26
139
SW 7000
Ibis White
SW 7001
Marshmallow
SW 7002
Downy
SW 7003
Toque White
pale celery
WHITE DUCK SW7010
lemon ice
powder sand
OC-113
Raindrop White
30GG 83/006
CN30
33-9
RD-W5
Moonlit Beach
NT24
NT24
PPG14-24 Dogwood Blossom
29
SW 6196
Frosty White
SW 6197
Aloof Gray
SW 6198
Sensible Hue
TIBETAN JASMINE • RL4011
WN30
Parchment White
60YY 83/062
BENJAMIN MOORE®
COLOR PREVIEW®
SW 6197
Aloof Gray
Frosty White
white dove
7002-18

Chapter 8

THE BUCKET LIST

Nothing revives an accessory, a room, or even a whole house quite like a fresh coat of paint—especially when that paint is a dreamy neutral. Enter the definitive guide to white (and almost-white) paint colors. From stark to soulful, warm to cool toned, these hues are editor tested and decorater approved. Whether you're on the hunt for a bleached-out shade to coat your walls or a creamy hue to reinvigorate an old piece of furniture, these no-fail colors will have you covered. Plus, tips and tricks for selecting the perfect finish, application, and more.

WARM UNDERTONES

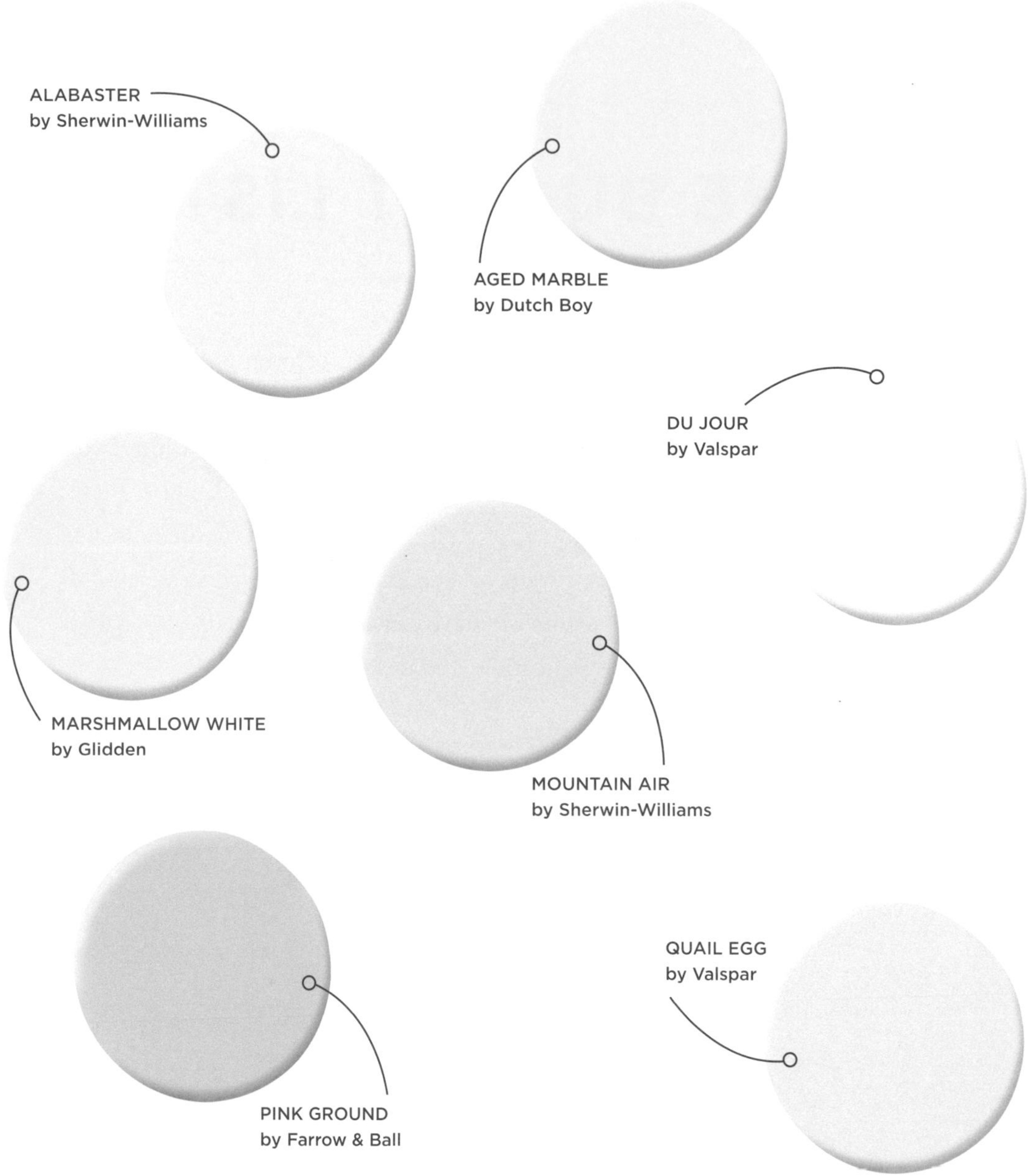

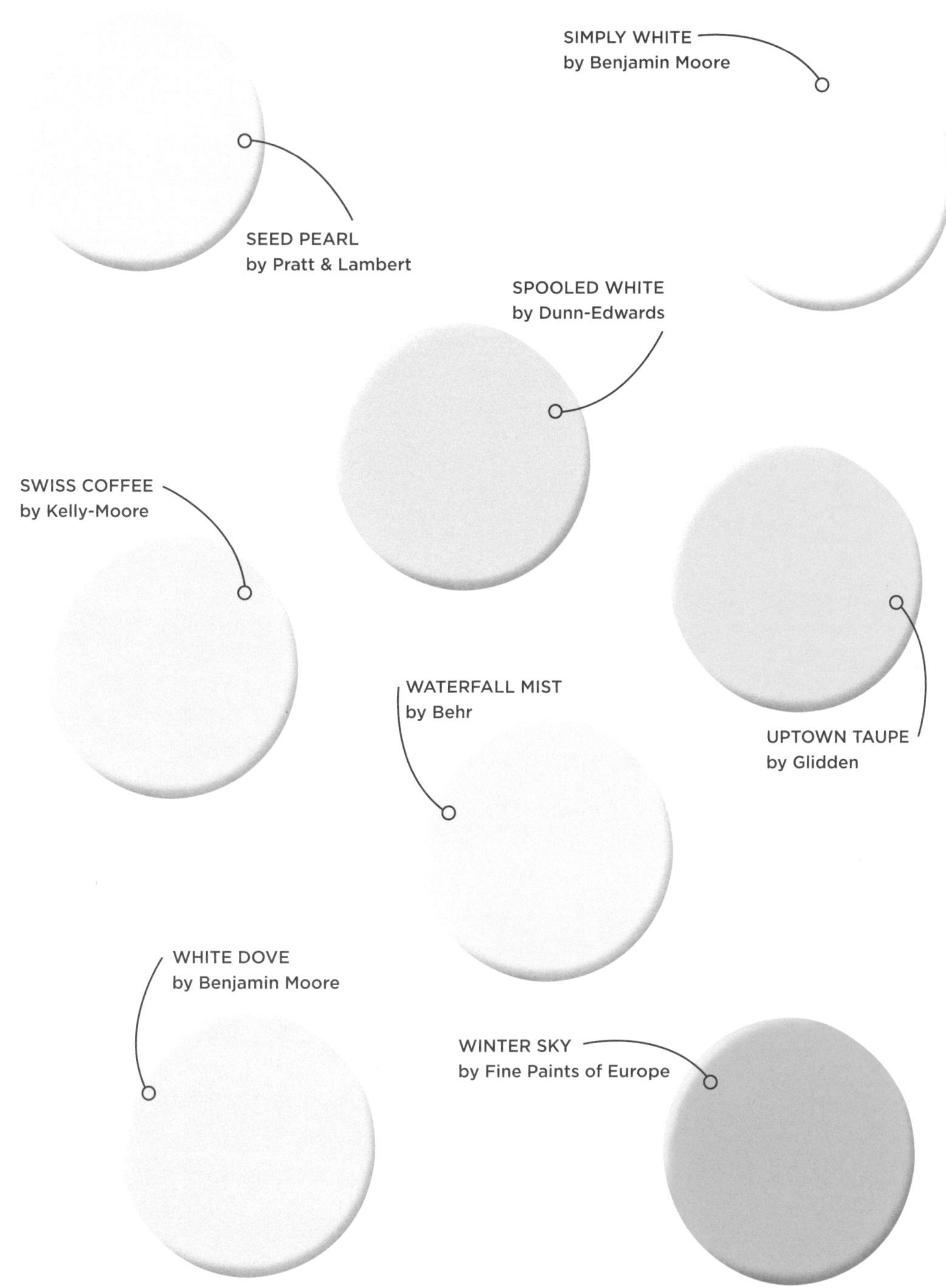
SIMPLY WHITE
by Benjamin Moore
SEED PEARL
by Pratt & Lambert
SPOOLED WHITE
by Dunn-Edwards
SWISS COFFEE
by Kelly-Moore
UPTOWN TAUPE
by Glidden
WATERFALL MIST
by Behr
WHITE DOVE
by Benjamin Moore
WINTER SKY
by Fine Paints of Europe

COOL UNDERTONES

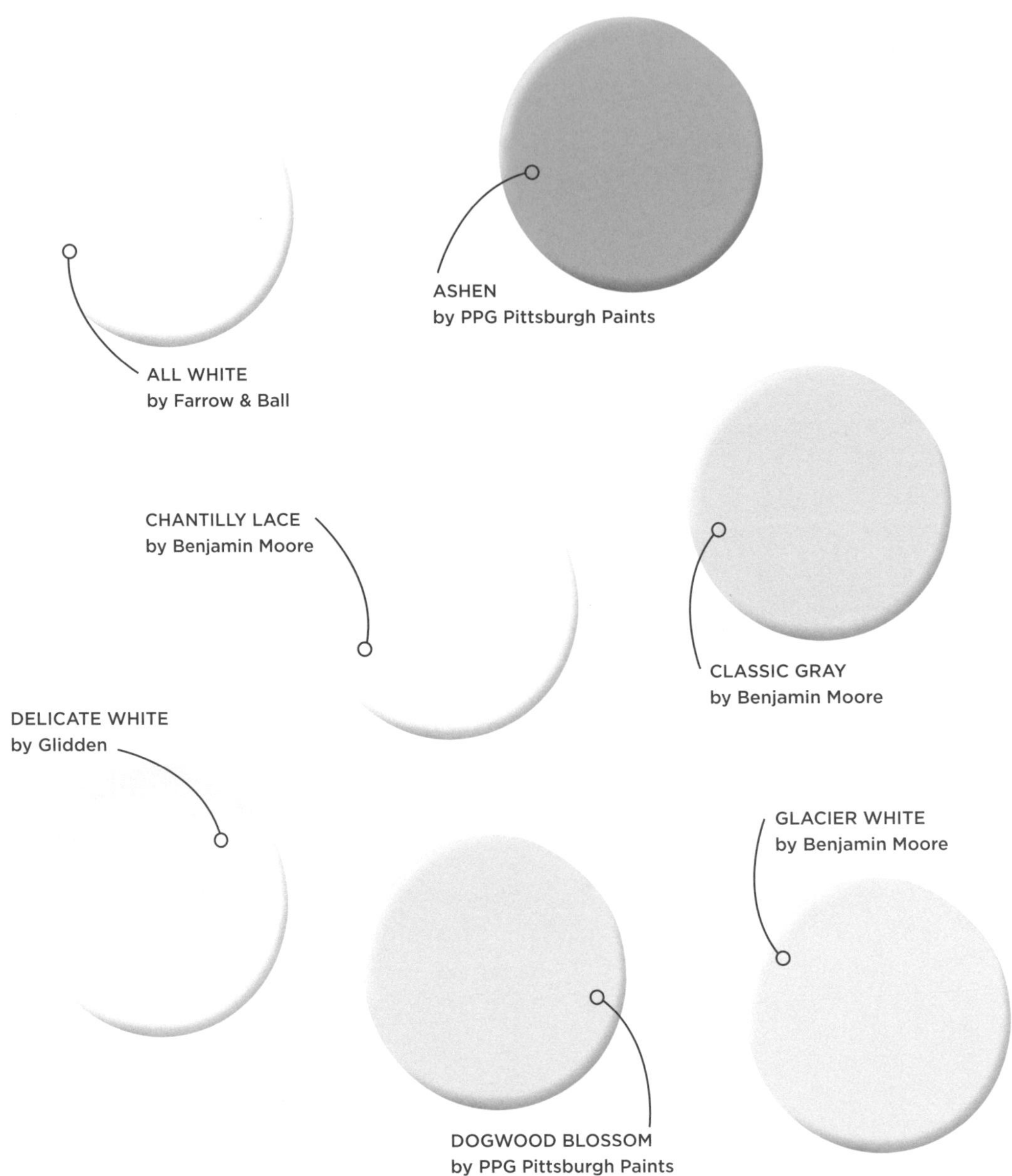

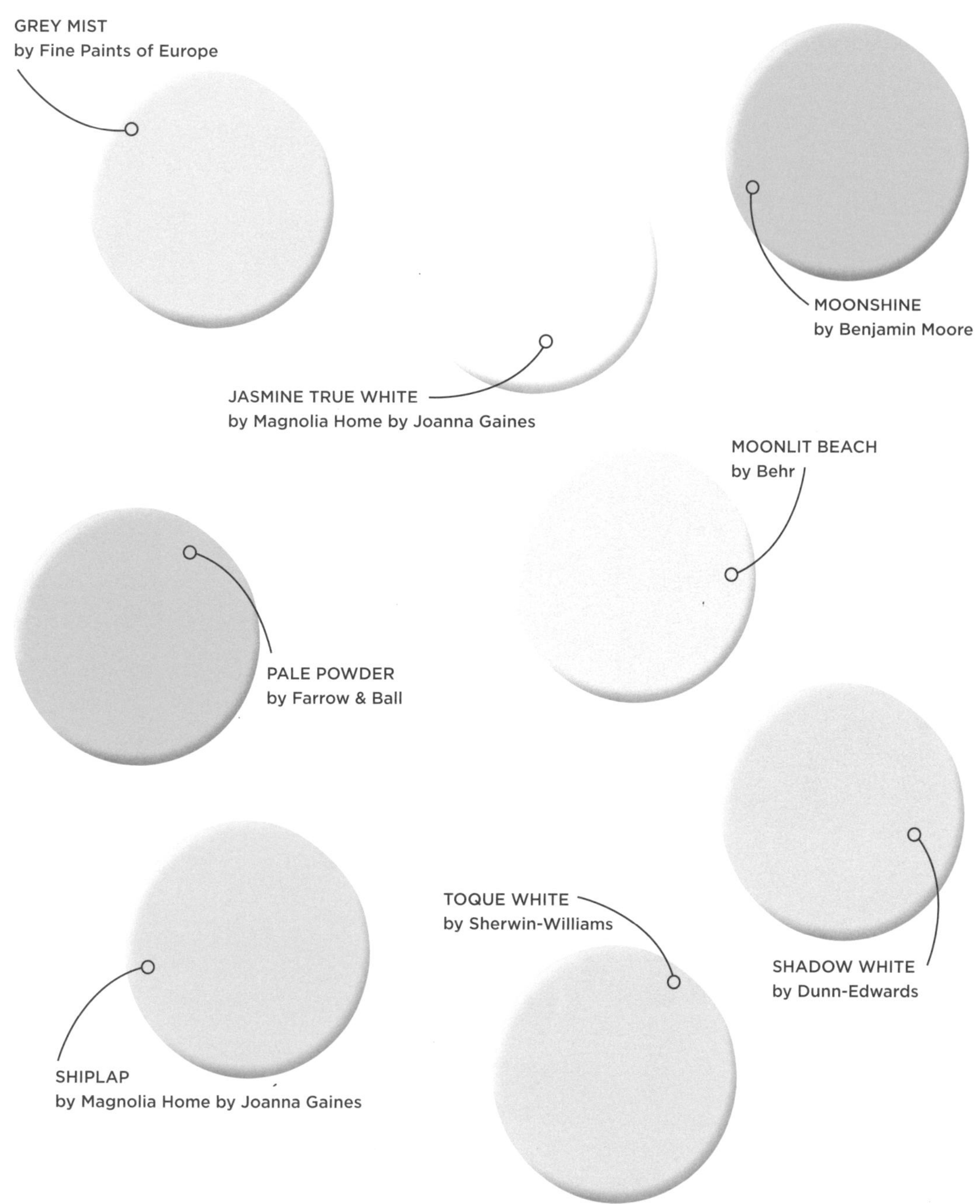
GREY MIST
by Fine Paints of Europe
MOONSHINE
by Benjamin Moore
JASMINE TRUE WHITE
by Magnolia Home by Joanna Gaines
MOONLIT BEACH
by Behr
PALE POWDER
by Farrow & Ball
TOQUE WHITE
by Sherwin-Williams
SHADOW WHITE
by Dunn-Edwards
SHIPLAP
by Magnolia Home by Joanna Gaines

Spray-Paint Makeovers

When in doubt, break out the white spray paint! The hardware store staple can transform flea-market finds or junk-closet castoffs into decidedly chic pieces. Behold these before and afters.

Spray-Paint Pointers

1. Opt for an all-purpose spray paint that's made to work on every surface from glossy ceramic to wood to fabric. Also, try a matte variety for its milky, not-so-lacquered effect.

2. Keep your distance . . . A good rule of thumb: Hold the nozzle twelve inches from the item for the most even finish. (Don't try this indoors!)

3. . . . And keep moving. Avoid lingering too long on any one area. Instead, stay in constant motion to avoid drips.

4. Be patient. Most of the items shown here required two to three coats of paint and dried for about forty-five minutes between each.

5. Don't save it for a rainy day. Achieving an even application can be challenging in humidity.

Paint Primer: Choosing a Paint Finish

Here's what you need to know about the five main paint finishes:

FLAT PAINT is also known as matte finish and has the least amount of shine. Because it doesn't reflect light, it's the best choice to hide imperfections like bumps or small cracks on walls. It also goes on smoother over rough surfaces, so it's a good option for textured walls. It's harder to keep clean and, therefore, not recommended for high-traffic areas.

EGGSHELL PAINT is the perfect finish for standard drywall. Sometimes called satin finish, eggshell has slightly more luster than a flat finish, but you won't be left with shiny walls. It resists stains better than flat and can be wiped clean with a wet rag.

SEMI-GLOSS PAINT is tougher than eggshell so it will show less wear. It reflects even more light when dry, though, so any imperfections on your walls before you paint will stand out afterward. This finish is often used for trim, doors, and furniture.

GLOSS PAINT is typically reserved for window and door trim, though you will sometimes find an entire room coated in it for a dramatic, glam effect. It's also a great choice for furniture because of its hard and shiny finish.

CHALK-FINISH PAINT is a term coined by paint maven Annie Sloan in the 1990s and has become synonymous with paints with a matte—almost chalky—look. It's now beloved for painting furniture—the thick finish gives pieces, both old and new, a timeworn look. *Bonus:* It requires virtually zero priming or sanding.

PHOTOGRAPHY CREDITS

COVER

Cover photographs by /shutterstock.com *(front)*; Annie Schlechter *(back)*

INTERIOR

© Lucas Allen: 13, 40, 44, 49, 145

© Jean Allsopp: 61

© Mali Azima: 150, 156

Courtesy Ballarddesigns.com: 25 (check)

© Christopher Baker: 147

© Lincoln Barbour: 3 (kitchen), 16, 17, 19, 75, 83, 84

© Stacey Brandford: 157, 158

© Monica Buck: 38

© Marta Xo Chilt: 8

© Jonn Coolidge: 131

© Paul Costello: 163

© Grey Crawford: 63

Courtesy Dashandalbert.com: 21 (sisal)

© Roger Davies: 54, 82, 166

© Jenna Diermann: 22

© Tara Donne: 60, 86

© Lisa Freedman: 155

© Philip Ficks: 137

© Philip Ficks with Homeowners—Jesse James and Kostas Anagnopoulos, of Aesthetic Movement 59

© Dana Gallagher: 167

© Tria Giovan: 29, 112

© Gridley & Graves: 120, 136, 149

© John Gruen: 68, 124, 168

Courtesy Guildery.com: 25 (graphic)

© Alec Hemmer: 6, 58, 81, 164

© Aimee Herring: 142

© Kat Hertzler: 26

© David Hillegas: 27 (coffee table), 97, 170, 176—177

Courtesy Johnrobshaw.com: 25 (floral)

© Max Kim-Bee: 11, 24, 45, 46, 47, 70, 73, 78, 79, 85, 92, 93, 104, 106, 109, 110, 111, 113, 114, 117, 126, 129, 135, 138

© David Land: 9, 102, 139

© Ray Kachatorian 178

© Charles Maraia: 74

© Andrew McCaul: 37

© Andrew McCaul & Catherine Gratwicke: ii, 31

© James Merrell: 134

© Karyn Millet: 30, 132

© Leslee Mitchell: 160, 161

© Keith Scott Morton: 23, 64, 65, 165

© Laura Moss: 41, 140

© Nancy Nolan: 28

© Helen Norman: 20, 56

Courtesy Overstock.com: 21 (seagrass)

© Victoria Pearson: 32, 33, 43, 77, 96, 98, 105, 107, 118, 130

© Jose Picayo: 146

© Lisa Romerein: 52, 53, 57

© Annie Schlechter: 5, 34, 36, 42, 89, 99, 100, 101, 108, 115, 116, 125, 141, 148, 153

Courtesy Shopsocietysocial.com: 21 (jute)

Shutterstock.com: wk1003mike iv

© James Salomon: 35

© Tim Street-Porter: 10

© Buff Strickland: 51, 159

© Robin Stubbert: 7 (table), 127

Courtesy Surefit.com: 25 (stripe)

© David Tsay: 2, 4, 14, 18, 88, 91, 94, 95, 103, 133

© Cody Ulrich: 169

© Dominque Vorillon: 67, 72, 122

© Bjorn Wallander: 11, 50, 66, 71, 80, 121, 128

© William Waldron: 62

© Julian Wass: 48

© Brian Woodcock: 3 (cupboard), 7 (bed room), 55, 76, 90, 151, 152

© Andrea Wyner: vi, 123

© Cody Ulrich: 27 (couch)

INDEX